THE MAGNIFICENT

BOOK

OF

INSECTS AND SPIDERS

THE
MAGNIFICENT
❖ BOOK ❖
OF
INSECTS AND SPIDERS

ILLUSTRATED BY
Val Walerczuk

WRITTEN BY
Barbara Taylor

Written by Barbara Taylor
Illustrated by Val Walerczuk
Additional Illustrations by Simon Mendez

Published by Weldon Owen Children's Books
An imprint of Weldon Owen International, L.P.
A subsidiary of Insight International, L.P.
PO Box 3088
San Rafael, CA 94912
www.insighteditions.com

Weldon Owen Children's Books:
Designed by Bryn Walls
Edited by Diana Craig
Senior Production Manager: Greg Steffen
Art Director: Stuart Smith
Publisher: Sue Grabham

Insight Editions:
Publisher: Raoul Goff

ISBN: 978-1-68188-773-9
Printed and bound in China
25 24 23 22 2 3 4 5

 # Introduction

From forests, deserts, marshlands, and streams to fields, city streets, and people's homes, insects and spiders live in almost every corner of the world. They have existed on our planet for over 300 million years, long before dinosaurs or people. Today, there are over five million species of insect and more than 50,000 species of spider.

Insects and spiders both have a tough outer shell, like a suit of armor, but they are different in other important ways. Insects have six legs and most have wings and can fly. Spiders have eight legs and are wingless.

The Magnificent Book of Insects and Spiders introduces you to some of the world's most amazing examples of these small creatures. Meet a beetle that is as heavy as an apple and a spider that spins a golden web. See a wasp that looks like an ant and find out how a killer bug breathes underwater.

Meet the deadly masters of disguise, such as the insect that looks like an orchid and the spider that can change color. Learn the tricks others use to stay safe, such as the moth that imitates a deadly snake and the stick insect that looks like crumpled leaves.

Discover these fascinating facts and many more as you zoom in on the magnificent miniature world of insects and spiders.

Fact file

Some of the information in the fact files in this book is different for insects and spiders:

Length: The length of an insect, including its head and body.

Legspan: The widest measurement across a spider's legs.

Lifecycle: The complete length of an insect's life, through all its stages of development: egg, larva (young), pupa, and adult; or egg, nymph (young), and adult.

Lifespan: The total length of a spider's life, from when it hatches from an egg as a spiderling.

Contents

Goliath beetle

Goliathus goliatus

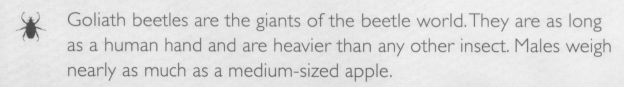

- Goliath beetles are the giants of the beetle world. They are as long as a human hand and are heavier than any other insect. Males weigh nearly as much as a medium-sized apple.

- The male goliath beetle has Y-shaped horns on his head. He uses his horns to fight for food or compete for mates.

- Females have wedge-shaped heads. They use them to burrow underground to lay their eggs.

- Fat, white, wrinkled grubs hatch out of the beetle's eggs. They have no eyes because they live in the dark underground.

The goliath grub eats rotting wood, plant material, and dung. It gets so big that eventually it weighs twice as much as the adult beetle.

 The grub builds a coccoon around itself underground and slowly changes into an adult beetle inside. When the adult comes out, it sleeps underground until the start of the dry season.

 For their size, these big beetles climb well. They use their sharp claws to cling to trees, branches, and vines in the rainforest.

Fact file

Lives: Western, eastern, and southern Africa

Habitat: Tropical rainforest

Length: 2–4 in/5–10 cm (adult); 10 in/25 cm (larva)

Lifecycle: 6 to 12 months

Diet: Tree sap, ripe fruit, dung, wood, dead leaves

Blue morpho butterfly

Morpho peleides

- The blue morpho's wings are formed of up to a million tiny, pyramid-shaped scales, which overlap, like the tiles on a roof. The scales reflect light so that the wings shimmer with dazzling color.

- The morpho has huge wings. Together, they measure up to 8 in (20 cm) across, which is longer than a man's hand.

- Male blue morphos have brighter blue wings than the females. They flash them to scare off rival males and to show off to the females.

- Morphos have brown underwings. With their wings closed, the butterflies are hard for birds and other predators to spot.

Fact file

Lives: Central and South America

Habitat: Tropical rainforest

Length: 6 in/15 cm

Lifecycle: 4 to 6 months

Diet: Leaves (caterpillar); fruit, tree sap, juices of dead animals (butterfly)

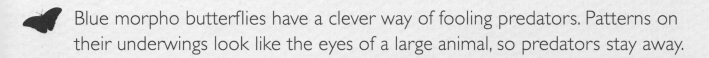 Blue morpho butterflies have a clever way of fooling predators. Patterns on their underwings look like the eyes of a large animal, so predators stay away.

When it is threatened, this butterfly gives off a stinky smell from its front legs.

Morpho caterpillars sometimes turn into cannibals and eat each other. This may happen if there isn't enough food to go round.

Spiny leaf stick insect

Extatosoma tiaratum

 This stick insect looks more like old, crumpled leaves than sticks or twigs. It sways to and fro in the wind, the way real leaves do. This clever disguise protects it from predators.

 The female has tiny wings and is too big to fly. Thorn-like spikes on her body protect her from predators. The male has long wings and can fly away from danger.

If threatened, the stick insect curls its tail over its back, so it looks like a deadly scorpion. It also gives off a horrible smell.

 A female stick insect can reproduce by herself, without a mate. All her babies will be female.

 Red-headed black ants often carry the stick insect's eggs back to their burrow. They eat the little edible caps on the top of each egg. This doesn't harm the eggs, and provides them with a safe place to hatch.

Fact file

Lives: Northeastern Australia

Habitat: Forest and grassland

Length: 8 in/20 cm (female); 4 in/10 cm (male)

Lifecycle: Up to 2 years

Diet: Eucalyptus and other leaves

Flower crab spider

Misumena vatia

 The flower crab spider does not spin a silk web or wrap its prey in silk like many other spiders. The male catches a few small flies as he moves about, but the female sits very still on a flower and waits to ambush her victims.

 Female flower crab spiders can change color to match the yellow or white color of the flowers they are sitting on. This helps to hide them from both prey and predators. It can take up to twenty days to change color completely.

 The male spiders are mainly dark brown, white, or green. They spend most of their time jumping from flower to flower looking for females.

Fact file

Lives: Europe and North America

Habitat: Woodland, grassland, scrubland, gardens

Legspan: 1¼ in/32 mm (female); ½–¾ in/16 mm (male)

Lifespan: Up to 2 years

Diet: Insects (male and female); flower pollen (male)

The spider's front two pairs of legs are longer and stronger than its other legs. It holds them open, ready to trap and grip its victims.

 Using its small jaws, the spider injects venom into its prey. The venom paralyzes, or numbs, the victim in just a few seconds. This helps the spider to overcome prey much larger than itself, such as bees.

 The flower crab spider holds tightly onto its prey and sucks its body dry.

 This spider has a short, wide, flat body and can walk sideways and backward like a real crab. It also holds its legs out at the sides of its body, in the same way as crabs do.

Giant stag beetle

Lucanus elaphus

- The huge jaws of the male giant stag beetle give this insect its name. They look like the antlers of a male deer, or stag.

- The male uses his massive jaws for fighting other males. The winner gets to mate with the females.

The female's tiny "antlers" are no use for defense, but she gives a sharp bite if attacked. The male can only give a nip despite his giant jaws.

The stag beetle has delicate wings. These stay tucked away under its hard brown wing cases until the beetle wants to fly. Males fly more than females, in their search for mates.

Female giant stag beetles lay their eggs inside the soft, damp wood of dead and decaying trees. The big white grubs that hatch out of the eggs feed on the rotting wood for up to three years.

Stag beetle grubs help trees to grow and forests to survive. As they feed on dead wood, they break it down, releasing the nutrients it contains into the soil.

Fact file

Lives: Eastern North America

Habitat: Damp deciduous forests

Length: 1¾–2¼ in/45–60 mm (male); 1–1¼ in/30–35 mm (female)

Lifecycle: 4 years 3 weeks

Diet: Rotten wood (grub); plant juices, rotting fruit, aphid honeydew (beetle)

Lantern bug

Pyrops candelaria

❧ People once believed that the extra-long head of this insect could glow in the dark, so they called it "lantern" bug. They were wrong—lantern bugs do not give off any light.

❧ Lantern bugs live high up in the rainforest, on trees such as lychee and mango.

❧ The lantern bug pierces tree bark with the sharp, needle-like mouthparts under its red "horn." It sucks up the sweet sap flowing beneath the bark.

❧ To attract females, males show off their dancing skills. They stretch and shake their back legs and sway their bodies from side to side.

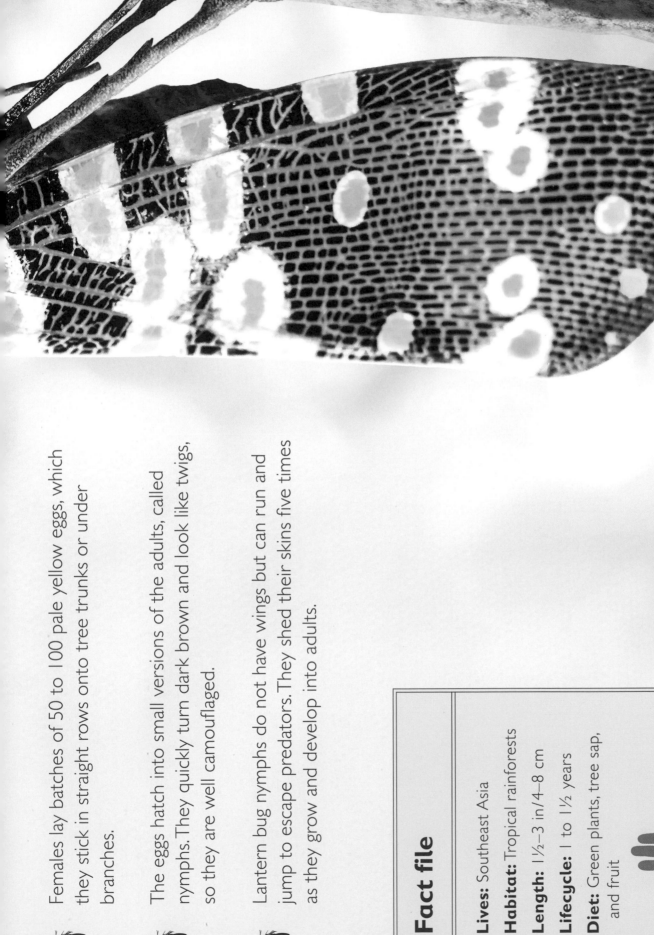

- Females lay batches of 50 to 100 pale yellow eggs, which they stick in straight rows onto tree trunks or under branches.

- The eggs hatch into small versions of the adults, called nymphs. They quickly turn dark brown and look like twigs, so they are well camouflaged.

- Lantern bug nymphs do not have wings but can run and jump to escape predators. They shed their skins five times as they grow and develop into adults.

Fact file

Lives: Southeast Asia

Habitat: Tropical rainforests

Length: 1½–3 in/4–8 cm

Lifecycle: 1 to 1½ years

Diet: Green plants, tree sap, and fruit

Human flea

Pulex irritans

The human flea is a champion jumper. It can jump up to 150 times its height, which is like a human leaping over a building taller than a house. The flea jumps onto animals as they pass by.

Fleas have little elastic pads on their back legs, which catapult them into the air. They can bounce back up again straight away.

Adult human fleas use their piercing and sucking mouthparts to feed on the blood of large mammals such as people, dogs, cats, sheep, and cattle.

An adult flea eats up to 10 to 15 blood meals in one day, but it can survive for one or two weeks without eating.

Fact file

Lives: Worldwide (except Arctic)

Habitat: Large mammals, homes, farms, animals' nests

Length: less than ¼ in/2.5–3.5 mm (female); less than ¼ in 2–2.5 mm (male)

Lifecycle: 1 month to more than 2 years

Diet: Blood (adult); flea droppings (larva)

A female flea needs a meal of blood before she can lay eggs. She lays 20 to 50 eggs a day, or 2,000 eggs in her lifetime.

The flea's lifecycle from egg to adult may take only three or four weeks, but can last much longer. Adult fleas live for two to three months.

Human fleas are so tiny that they look like black specks to us. The larvae, or grubs, look like maggots and have no legs or eyes.

Jumping spider

Bagheera kiplingi

 Most spiders are meat-eaters, but this jumping spider is mostly vegetarian. It eats the swollen tips of acacia leaves and feeds on plant nectar. Sometimes it snacks on insects too.

 This fast, agile jumping spider uses its powerful legs to jump up to fifty times its own body length.

This jumping spider was named after Bagheera, the black panther in the *Jungle Book*, written by Rudyard Kipling. Bagheera was good at jumping.

 The *Bagheera* spider lives on acacia trees alongside fierce ants that live there too. Despite this, the cunning spider manages to steal some of the sugary leaf tips that the ants break off to eat.

 To avoid being attacked by the ants that it lives with, the spider often leaps onto a nearby leaf or drops down suddenly. It clings to a safety line made from its own silk so that it can pull itself back up.

 Like most other spiders, this jumping spider has eight eyes, including two big eyes, which look like car headlamps. Scientists think it may be able to see more colors than humans can.

 Male jumping spiders dance to attract females and may help to care for the eggs and young.

Fact file

Lives: Central America

Habitat: Tropical forests

Legspan: ¼ in/6–8 mm

Lifespan: 1 year

Diet: Acacia leaf tips, nectar, flies, ant larvae

Leafcutter ant

Atta cephalotes

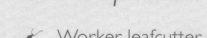 Worker leafcutter ants use their powerful, scissor-like mouthparts to snip pieces off the leaves of trees. They make the leaves into a compost for growing a special kind of fungus, which they eat.

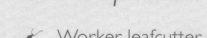 Leafcutter ants hold their leaves up in the air like the sails on a boat. They grip them using the spines on their backs and a groove on their heads.

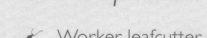 Smaller workers sometimes hitch a ride on the leaves carried by larger workers. They clean the leaves and chase off any flies that try to lay their eggs on the larger workers' heads.

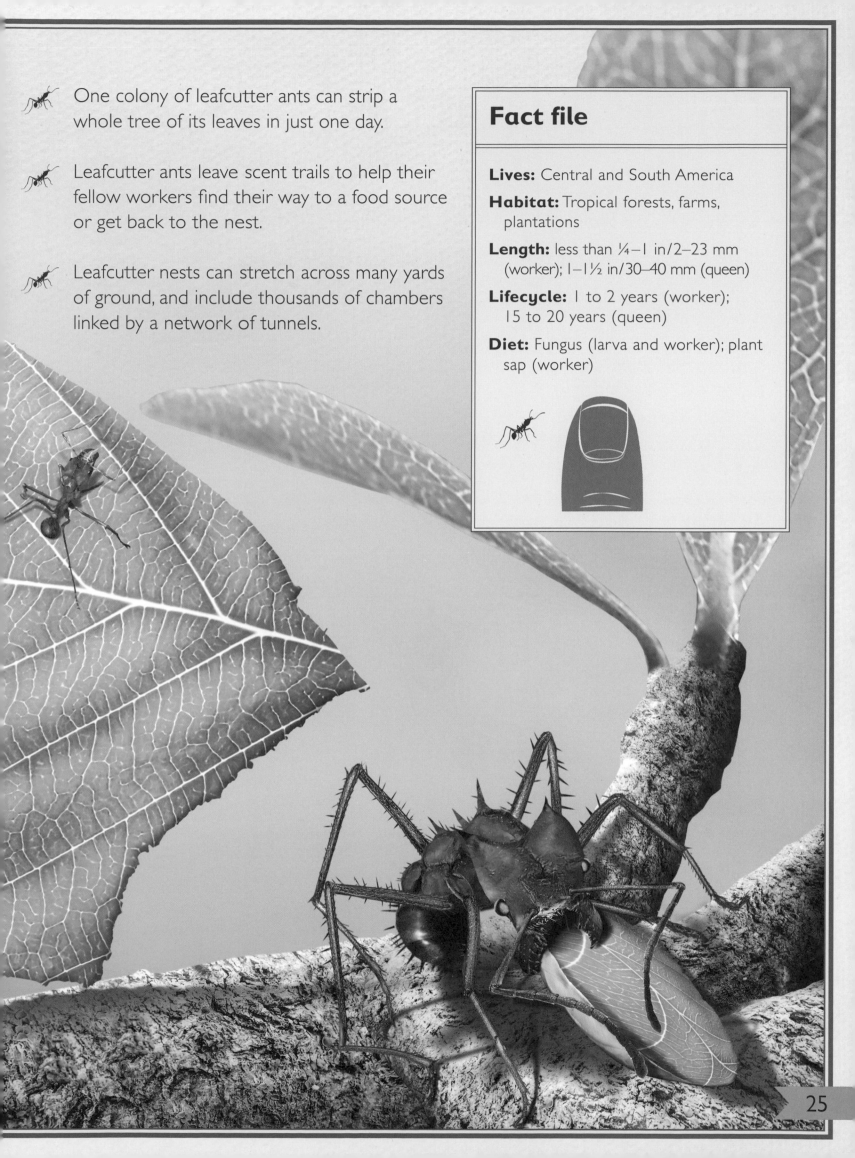

One colony of leafcutter ants can strip a whole tree of its leaves in just one day.

Leafcutter ants leave scent trails to help their fellow workers find their way to a food source or get back to the nest.

Leafcutter nests can stretch across many yards of ground, and include thousands of chambers linked by a network of tunnels.

Fact file

Lives: Central and South America

Habitat: Tropical forests, farms, plantations

Length: less than ¼–1 in/2–23 mm (worker); 1–1½ in/30–40 mm (queen)

Lifecycle: 1 to 2 years (worker); 15 to 20 years (queen)

Diet: Fungus (larva and worker); plant sap (worker)

Western honey bee

Apis mellifera

- Honey bees have a tongue with a brush-like tip for soaking up the sweet, liquid nectar from flowers. They turn the nectar into honey, which they eat and also feed to their larvae, or young.

- A honey bee colony contains 20,000 to 60,000 individuals. Most are female workers. There are hundreds of male drones too, but they die after mating. The single queen bee lays all the eggs.

- Young worker honey bees are taught how to make honey by older bees in the hive.

- The worker bees produce wax inside their bodies. Tiny flakes of this wax ooze out from under their abdomens. The workers chew the wax and use it to build honeycombs made of six-sided cells.

- A honey bee has to collect nectar from about two million flowers to produce 1 lb (450 g) honey, which is enough to fill a jar.

- Honey bees dance to pass messages to each other. Their "waggle dance" shows the bees where to find flowers with lots of nectar.

- The buzzing sound that bees make comes from their wings, which beat at 12,000 to 15,000 times a minute.

- The female workers and queens can sting because their sting is a kind of egg-laying tube. The worker bees can only sting once but the queens can sting many times.

- A honey bee's sense of smell is fifty times more powerful than a dog's sense of smell. It can see every color except red.

Fact file

Lives: Worldwide (except Antarctica)

Habitat: Trees, caves, manmade hives

Length: ½ in/13 mm (worker); ¾ in/20 mm (queen)

Lifecycle: 6 to 9 weeks (worker); up to 5 years (queen)

Diet: Flower nectar (adult and larva); flower pollen (larva)

Monarch butterfly

Danaus plexippus

- Monarch butterflies are epic travelers. To escape the cold winter in Canada, thousands fly south to Mexico and California, around 3,000 miles (5,000 kilometers) away. In spring, monarchs fly north again.

- In Mexico, millions of monarchs roost together in fir or pine trees over the winter. Their wings are up to 4 in (10 cm) wide, and look like big, fluttering orange leaves.

- In her lifetime, a female monarch will lay 300 to 500 pinhead-size eggs. She glues each egg to a milkweed leaf. The eggs hatch after about four days.

Fact file

Lives: North America, Pacific Islands, Australia, New Zealand, Spain, Portugal

Habitat: Forests, mountains, fields, marshes, roadsides

Length: 2¼ in/7 cm (caterpillar); 1–1¾ in/25–46 mm (butterfly)

Lifecycle: 6 weeks to 9 months

Diet: Milkweed leaves (caterpillar); flower nectar (butterfly)

It takes a monarch caterpillar less than five minutes to eat one milkweed leaf. As it feeds, the caterpillar sheds its skin five times to allow it to grow bigger. It eats the old skins.

The caterpillar takes in poisons from the milkweed leaves it eats. These poisons stay in its body, even when it turns into an adult butterfly.

The monarch's bright colors are a warning to predators that it is poisonous and tastes nasty.

Pollution, disease, climate change, and habitat loss all threaten monarch butterflies with extinction. They need plenty of milkweed plants to eat if they are to survive.

American cockroach

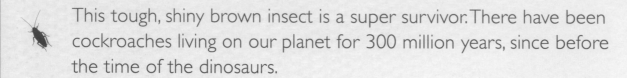

Periplaneta americana

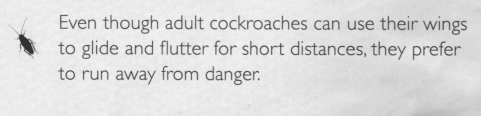

- This tough, shiny brown insect is a super survivor. There have been cockroaches living on our planet for 300 million years, since before the time of the dinosaurs.

- American cockroaches will eat almost anything, from paper, leather, and wallpaper paste to fabric, soap, and even dead or wounded cockroaches.

- With their long legs, American cockroaches are very fast runners. This helps them to escape from their many predators, such as spiders, mantids, fish, frogs, lizards, rats, cats, and monkeys.

- Even though adult cockroaches can use their wings to glide and flutter for short distances, they prefer to run away from danger.

The American cockroach can squeeze through tiny gaps by flattening its bendy body and spreading its legs out to the side.

A female American cockroach lays her eggs in a hard egg case shaped like a purse. She lays 15 eggs in each case, and produces about 150 eggs in her lifetime.

American cockroaches use their antennae, or feelers, to smell the world around them. They also use them to detect the scents given off by other cockroaches.

Fact file

Lives: Worldwide

Habitat: Buildings, sewers, drains, wood piles, gardens

Length: 1¼–2 in/32–53 mm excluding antennae

Lifecycle: Up to 2 years

Diet: Food scraps, insects, decaying leaves, fungi

Broad-winged katydid

Microcentrum rhombifolium

- The broad-winged katydid is very well camouflaged when it sits on tree leaves. Its wings even have markings that look like leaf veins.

- Male katydids make loud clicks to attract females. They rub a sharp scraper on one front wing against a file-like ridge on the other front wing. Females answer with a weak clicking signal of their own.

- The male katykid repeats his noisy courtship song every two to four seconds. The gaps in his singing make it difficult for predators to pinpoint where he is.

Fact file

Lives: North America

Habitat: Woodlands

Length: 2–2½ in/5.2–6.3 cm

Lifecycle: Up to 1 year

Diet: Leaves, flowers, fruit

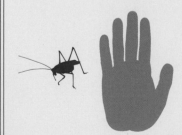

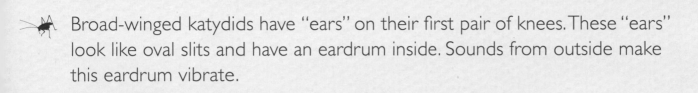 Broad-winged katydids have "ears" on their first pair of knees. These "ears" look like oval slits and have an eardrum inside. Sounds from outside make this eardrum vibrate.

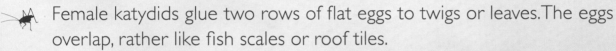 The broad-winged katydid uses its long, thread-like antennae to feel and smell its surroundings.

Female katydids glue two rows of flat eggs to twigs or leaves. The eggs overlap, rather like fish scales or roof tiles.

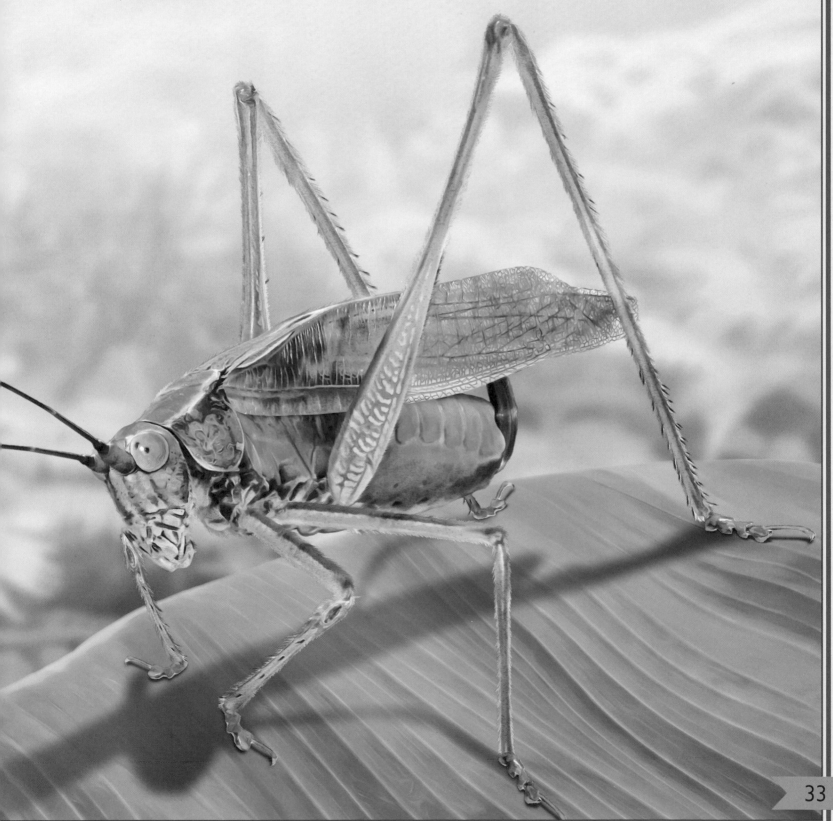

Asian giant hornet

Vespa mandarinia

- The fearsome Asian giant hornet is the world's biggest wasp. This thumb-sized insect is three times longer than a honeybee.

- The wasp's stripes warn predators that it has a large, poisonous sting, which it uses for defence. It can sting over and over again.

- Adult giant hornets cannot eat solid food so they drink the juices of the insects they catch. They also lick up the saliva that their grubs spit out.

- The adult wasps feed their grubs with a paste made from chewed-up prey.

Fact file

Lives: Eastern and Southeast Asia

Habitat: Lowland mountains and forests

Length: 1¼–1½ in/3.5–4 cm (worker); 1¾–2 in/4.5–5 cm (queen)

Lifecycle: 9 months (worker); 12 months (queen)

Diet: Bees, mantises, beetles, other hornets, tree sap

Asian giant hornets live together in underground colonies of several hundred individuals, including the queen, workers, and males.

Worker giant hornets collect food, protect the nest and take care of the young hornets.

Giant hornets can destroy a whole honeybee colony in a few hours, but Japanese bees fight back. They form a hot, dense, vibrating ball around each hornet and "cook" the invader to death.

Large copper dung beetle

Scarabaeus nigroaenus

Large copper dung beetles lay their eggs in elephant dung. Using their strong sense of smell, they can sniff out a fresh pile of dung soon after it leaves the elephant.

The beetles shape a small lump of elephant dung into a ball. The male uses his strong legs to push the ball quickly away from the dung pile.

Female dung beetles often hitch a ride on top of the dung ball as it is rolled along.

Copper dung beetles steer their dung balls in a straight line. They check where the sun is in the sky and use it to guide them.

Fact file

Lives: Southern Africa

Habitat: Grassland, forest

Length: 1–1¼ in/25–30 mm

Lifecycle: 2 to 3 years

Diet: Elephant dung

Large copper dung beetles bury their dung balls in soft soil. Using their shovel-shaped heads, they dig away the soil from under the ball so that the ball slowly slips down.

 The female lays a single egg in the dung ball. When the grub hatches out, it eats the dung. The adult beetles feed on liquids inside the dung.

Giant water bug

Lethocerus deyrollei

- A fierce, nighttime predator, this giant water bug grabs its prey with its powerful, hooked front legs.

- Giant water bugs are nicknamed "toe biters" because they can give people a painful bite.

- This giant water bug usually eats small fish or water insects, but also catches larger prey such as baby turtles.

- The water bug uses its dagger-like mouthparts to inject deadly saliva, or spit, into the prey. This slowly turns the prey's insides into a soupy liquid, which the bug sucks up.

- Adult giant water bugs use a snorkel-like tube on their behinds to breathe in air at the surface of the water.

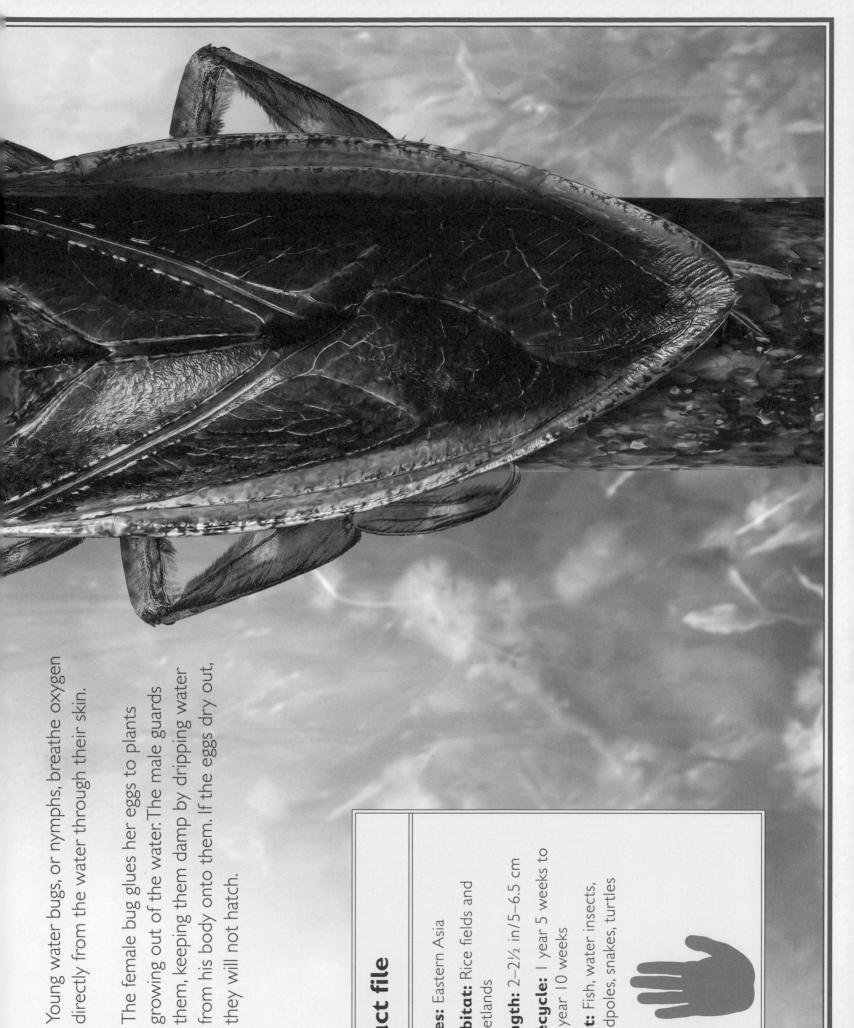

 Young water bugs, or nymphs, breathe oxygen directly from the water through their skin.

 The female bug glues her eggs to plants growing out of the water. The male guards them, keeping them damp by dripping water from his body onto them. If the eggs dry out, they will not hatch.

Fact file

Lives: Eastern Asia

Habitat: Rice fields and wetlands

Length: 2–2½ in/5–6.5 cm

Lifecycle: 1 year 5 weeks to 1 year 10 weeks

Diet: Fish, water insects, tadpoles, snakes, turtles

David Bowie huntsman spider

Heteropoda davidbowie

🕷 This hairy, orange huntsman spider is named after the rock star David Bowie, who dyed his hair bright orange and wore colorful clothes onstage.

🕷 The David Bowie spider has poor eyesight so cannot easily see its victims. Instead, it uses the long hairs on its legs to sense the vibrations caused by moving prey.

🕷 Instead of spinning a web to trap its meals, the huntsman stalks and chases prey. The spider's long legs help it to run very fast.

🕷 The huntsman spider can capture prey almost twice its size.

Fact file

Lives: Southeast Asia

Habitat: Tropical forest

Legspan: 4–5 in / 10–12 cm

Lifespan: About 2 years

Diet: Insects and spiders

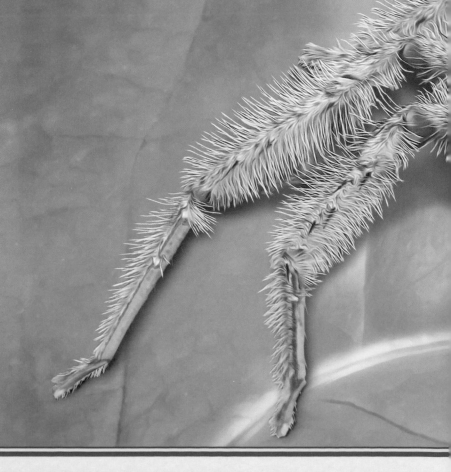

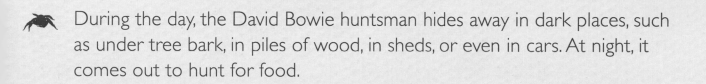 During the day, the David Bowie huntsman hides away in dark places, such as under tree bark, in piles of wood, in sheds, or even in cars. At night, it comes out to hunt for food.

The huntsman makes a daytime shelter out of strands of silk. It also spins silk safety lines when it is out and about. Then, if it falls, it can climb back up a safety line again.

The female David Bowie spider lays around 200 eggs at a time. She wraps them in an egg sac of white, papery silk, and does not eat for about three weeks while she is guarding them.

Red velvet ant

Dasymutilla occidentalis

- Red velvet ants were once nicknamed "cow killers" because people believed that the female's sting was powerful enough to kill a cow. This is not true, but her sting is painful and she can use it many times.

- Although they look like large, hairy ants, red velvet ants are really wasps. They live on their own and do not form colonies, like social wasps.

- The velvety hairs covering this wasp probably trap body moisture. This helps to stop it drying out in hot places.

- The wingless females speed along the ground on their powerful legs in search of a place to lay their eggs.

Fact file

Lives: North America, but also worldwide

Habitat: Deserts, meadows, fields, lawns

Length: ½–1 in / 15–25 mm

Lifecycle: 10 to 12 months

Diet: Bee and wasp larvae (grub); nectar (adult)

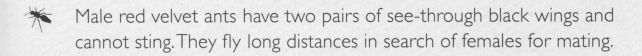 Male red velvet ants have two pairs of see-through black wings and cannot sting. They fly long distances in search of females for mating.

Female velvet ants lay their eggs in the nests of other solitary wasps or bees. When their larvae, or grubs, hatch out, they eat the other larvae in the nest.

If it is attacked or captured, the red velvet ant makes a loud squeaking noise. It does this by rubbing two different parts of its belly against each other.

Asian tiger mosquito

Aedes albopictus

- The fierce Asian tiger mosquito gets the "tiger" part of its name from its black-and-white stripes.

- Female tiger mosquitoes bite people and other animals to collect their blood. They need this blood to help their eggs develop.

- When the female mosquito bites, she stabs two sharp tubes into her victim. One tube sucks blood and the other tube injects saliva to keep the blood flowing.

- The male mosquitoes do not bite. Instead, they feed on flower nectar and other plant juices.

Fact file

Lives: Southeast Asia, Americas

Habitat: Forests, towns, cities, countryside

Length: up to ½ in/2–10 mm

Lifecycle: 4 to 6 weeks

Diet: Blood (female); plant juices and nectar (female and male)

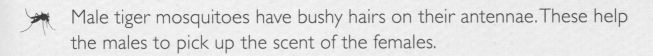 Male tiger mosquitoes have bushy hairs on their antennae. These help the males to pick up the scent of the females.

Female tiger mosquitoes lay their eggs about four or five days after drinking blood. One female can lay up to 500 eggs in her lifetime.

Tiger mosquito larvae develop into adults in as little as two weeks after hatching from the eggs.

As female tiger mosquitoes feed on blood, they may pass on the germs of serious human diseases, such as yellow fever, dengue fever, and the Zika virus.

Banded demoiselle

Calopteryx splendens

✳ The banded demoiselle is named after the dark band on the male's blue-green wings. The shiny green female does not have this band.

✳ When they rest, banded demoiselles hold their wings together over their body. They do not spread them out like dragonflies.

✳ Males dance in the air to show off their wings to attract females.

✳ The female lays her eggs on floating plants or injects them into stems underwater. She lays one egg every 2–6 seconds for about 45 minutes, using air trapped between her wings to breathe underwater.

✳ Banded demoiselle eggs hatch into stick-shaped larvae, or nymphs, underwater. They take two years to develop into adults.

✳ A demoiselle nymph has three long, feathery gills at the back of its body. It uses them to take in oxygen from the water, like a fish, while it is growing.

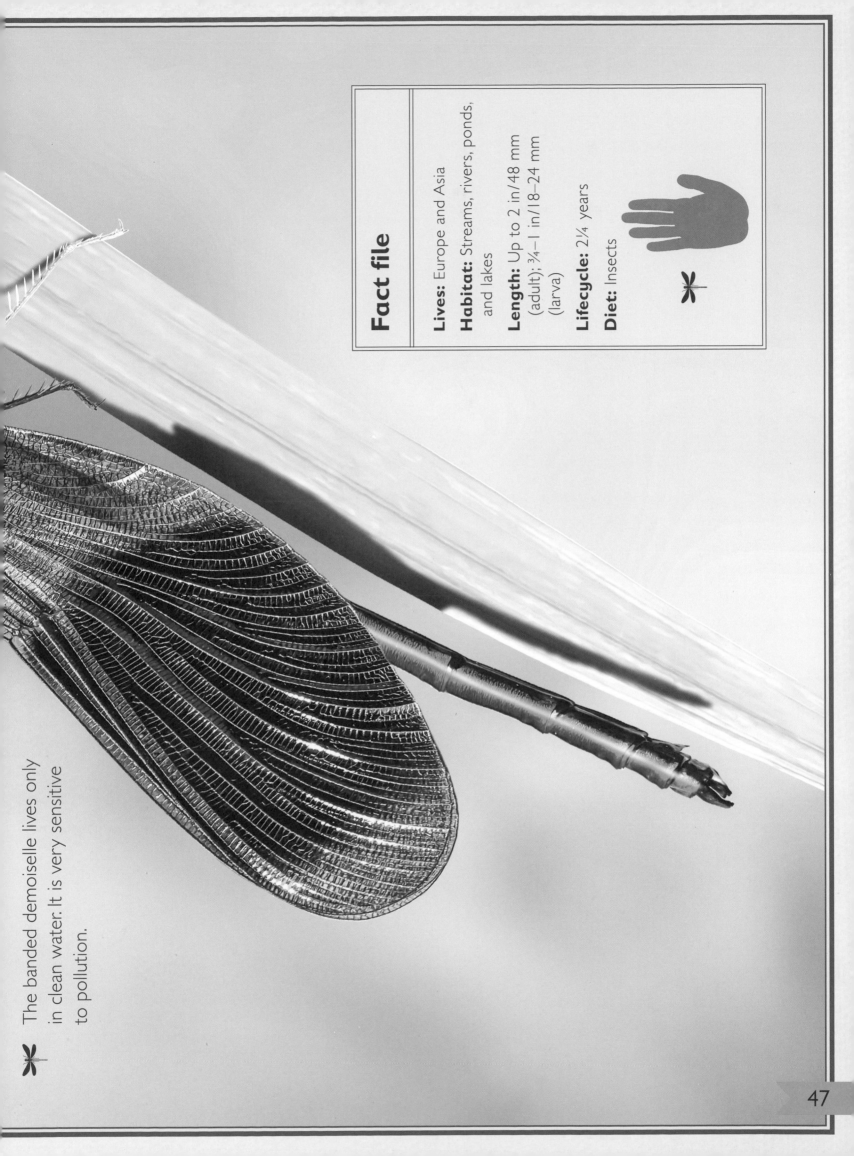

The banded demoiselle lives only in clean water. It is very sensitive to pollution.

Fact file

Lives: Europe and Asia

Habitat: Streams, rivers, ponds, and lakes

Length: Up to 2 in/48 mm (adult); ¾–1 in/18–24 mm (larva)

Lifecycle: 2¼ years

Diet: Insects

Giraffe weevil

Trachelophorus giraffa

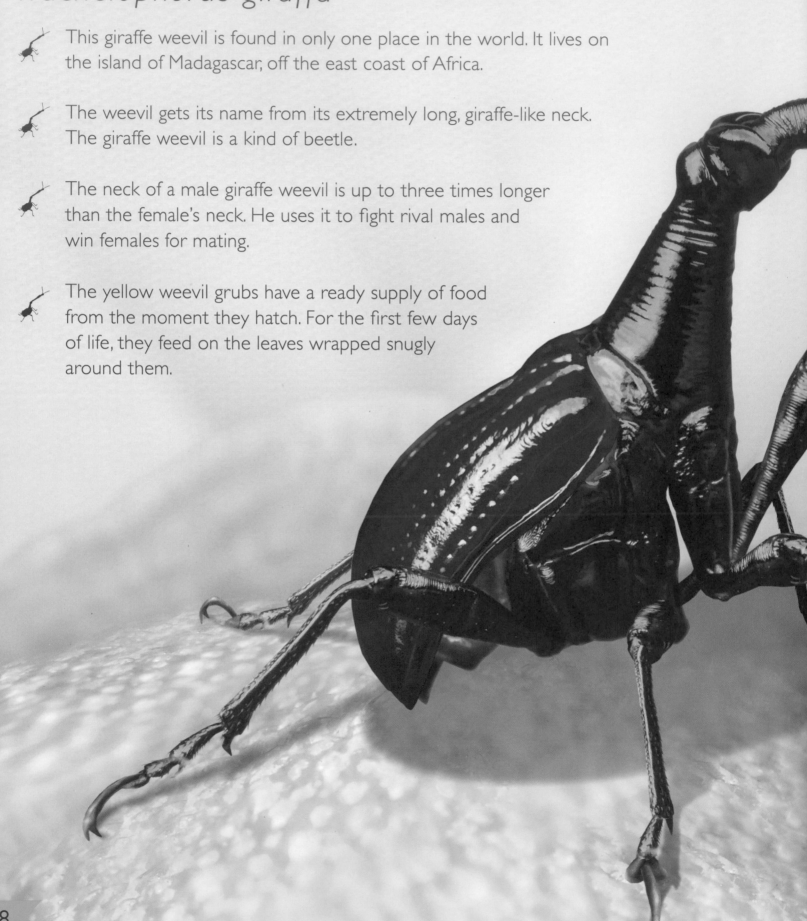

- This giraffe weevil is found in only one place in the world. It lives on the island of Madagascar, off the east coast of Africa.

- The weevil gets its name from its extremely long, giraffe-like neck. The giraffe weevil is a kind of beetle.

- The neck of a male giraffe weevil is up to three times longer than the female's neck. He uses it to fight rival males and win females for mating.

- The yellow weevil grubs have a ready supply of food from the moment they hatch. For the first few days of life, they feed on the leaves wrapped snugly around them.

Giraffe weevils spend most of their lives on the leaves of the giraffe beetle tree.

 The female weevil rolls up a large giraffe beetle leaf into a fat, tube-shaped parcel. She lays one egg inside the parcel, where it will be safe from predators. Then she snips the leaf away from the tree so it falls to the ground.

Fact file

Lives: Madagascar

Habitat: Rainforest

Length: 1 in/2.5 cm (male); ½ in/1.5 cm (female)

Lifecycle: From a few days to one year

Diet: Leaves of giraffe beetle tree

Atlas moth

Attacus atlas

The atlas moth is one of the largest moths in the world. The female is larger than the male and has a wingspan that is as wide as a dinner plate.

The name of the atlas moth is thought to come from the map-like patterns on its wings. A book of maps is called an atlas.

Female atlas moths release a scent to attract the males. The males use their feathery antennae to pick up this scent from several miles away.

The adult moths do not feed. They rely on large stores of fat built up during the hungry caterpillar stage to give them the energy they need to survive.

When it is threatened, the atlas moth drops to the floor and wriggles around. It slowly flaps its wings to imitate the movements of a snake. Its wing tips look like the head of a deadly cobra.

To protect themselves from predators, atlas moth caterpillars send out a spray of nasty-smelling liquids.

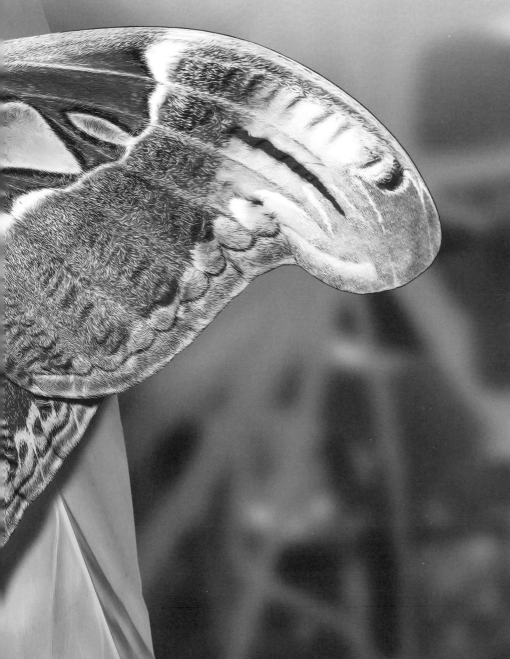

Fact file

Lives: Southeast Asia

Habitat: Tropical forests, shrubland

Length: 4¾ in/12 cm (caterpillar); 1½ in/4 cm (female); 1–1¼ in 3–3.6 cm (male)

Lifecycle: 11 to 14 weeks

Diet: Evergreen tree leaves (caterpillar)

Thailand black tarantula

Cyriopagopus minax

 This velvety black tarantula lives in deep, silk-lined burrows, which it makes on the rainforest floor. When prey trips over the silk threads around the entrance, the spider feels the vibrations and comes out to catch its victim.

If this tarantula is threatened, it raises its front legs to show off its venomous fangs. The tarantula may stay in this threat position for up to 20 minutes.

 The Thailand black tarantula has strong venom and it will bite to defend itself from danger. Its bite does not kill people, unless they are allergic to the venom.

 Like other tarantulas, this spider bites straight down, instead of using a sideways pinching movement of its fangs. This strong bite means that it can kill larger prey such as birds or frogs.

 Female Thailand black tarantulas may try to eat the males after mating. The males are smaller than the females.

Fact file

Lives: Southeast Asia

Habitat: Tropical rainforest

Legspan: 3–6 in/7.6–15 cm

Lifespan: 2 to 4 years (male); 11 to 13 years (female)

Diet: Birds, lizards, frogs, and insects

Aquatic firefly

Aquatica ficta

 Fireflies are not flies at all. They are a type of beetle.

 When it gets dark, the male aquatic firefly produces twinkling green lights to attract a female. He flashes his light signals as he flies along. If she is impressed by his display, the female answers with her own flashing lights.

 The firefly has an organ, or body part, just for making light. To create its flashing light, the firefly takes in oxygen from the air and mixes it with chemicals inside this organ.

 The larvae, or young, of aquatic fireflies live underwater for about a year. The adults live in the air for only two weeks—just long enough to mate and lay eggs.

 Firefly larvae are meat-eaters, but the adults are vegetarians, feeding on plant pollen and nectar. Sometimes the adults do not feed at all.

Fact file

Lives: Taiwan, China

Habitat: Still water, ponds, rice fields

Length: ¼–½ in/7–11 mm

Lifecycle: 388 days (55 weeks)

Diet: Water snails (larva); nectar, and pollen (adult)

 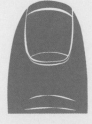

The blood of fireflies tastes bitter and is poisonous to some animals. This helps to protect them from predators.

 The bright lights of cities are harmful to fireflies. They make it harder for them to see each other's flashing light signals, find mates, and produce young.

 There are more than 2,000 species of firefly in the world. Only some can produce glowing lights, which can be yellow, green, or orange.

Golden silk spider

Trichonephila clavipes

🕷 The huge web of the female golden silk spider is one or two yards wide. Some of the silk threads are up to six times stronger than steel wire of the same thickness.

🕷 The yellow silk threads of the female's web shine like gold in the sunlight. The golden color may attract bees for the spider to eat.

🕷 Male golden silk spiders are five or six times smaller than the females and make much smaller webs. When they are ready to mate, they often perch on the edge of a female's web and may steal her food.

🕷 Female golden silk spiders bite their prey with venomous fangs to stop it moving. Then they wrap their meal in a silk-like cocoon and store it in the middle of their web until they are ready to eat.

🕷 The female spider lays her eggs inside an egg sac covered with curly yellow silk. There are hundreds of eggs inside each sac.

🕷 The golden silk spider is sometimes called the banana spider because its abdomen, or belly, is shaped like a banana.

Fact file

Lives: North, Central, and South America

Habitat: Forests, swamps

Legspan: Over 5 in/12 cm (female); ¾–1 in/2–2.4 cm (male)

Lifespan: Up to 1 year

Diet: Flying insects

Oak treehopper

Platycotis vittata

🐸 The oak treehopper lives in oak trees. If it is disturbed, it jumps up and flies to the next oak, which is why it is called a "tree hopper."

🐸 Treehoppers use their sharp beaks to pierce holes in the branches of oak trees. Then they suck up the sugary sap that flows underneath the bark.

🐸 These insects have a clever way of keeping sap flowing when they feed. They inject saliva, or spit, into the hole they have made in the bark. This stops the hole closing so they can continue sucking up the sap.

🐸 Oak treehoppers communicate by shaking their bodies. The vibrations travel through the branches and send messages to other treehoppers.

🐸 The oak treehopper usually has a hard, protective plate, or "helmet," at the front of its body. This looks like a thorn and helps to disguise the treehopper from predators.

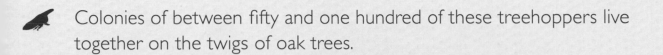 Colonies of between fifty and one hundred of these treehoppers live together on the twigs of oak trees.

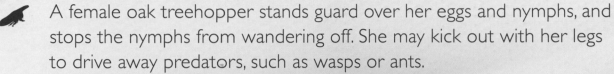 A female oak treehopper stands guard over her eggs and nymphs, and stops the nymphs from wandering off. She may kick out with her legs to drive away predators, such as wasps or ants.

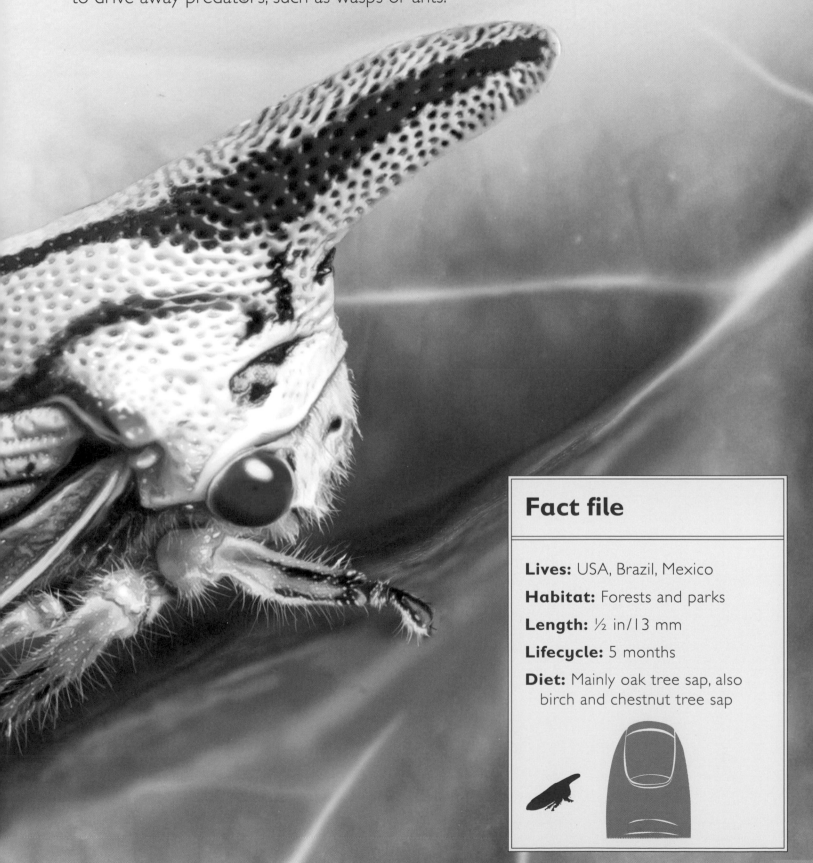

Fact file

Lives: USA, Brazil, Mexico

Habitat: Forests and parks

Length: ½ in/13 mm

Lifecycle: 5 months

Diet: Mainly oak tree sap, also birch and chestnut tree sap

Robber fly

Holcocephala fusca

- This tiny robber fly is as small as a grain of rice. It captures insects in flight, and is sometimes called the gnat ogre because it likes to eat flying gnats.

- The fly's super-sensitive goggle eyes are like high-power binoculars. They see very well but only over a narrow area.

- The robber fly attacks and captures its prey very rapidly, in about the time it would take you to blink twice.

- Hairy legs help the robber fly to latch onto its prey in flight.

- To paralyze and kill its victim, the robber fly injects it with poisonous saliva, or spit. The saliva also turns the inside of the prey into a liquid soup, which the robber fly drinks.

- The robber fly has two little drumstick-shaped lumps behind its wings. These are called halteres and help the insect to balance when flying.

Fact file

Lives: North America

Habitat: Grassy fields near woods

Length: up to ¼ in/5–7 mm

Lifecycle: 1 to 3 years

Diet: Small flying insects (adult); insect larvae, worms (grub)

Wheel bug

Arilus cristatus

🐜 Wheel bugs are named after their spiny, wheel-like crests. They are a type of assassin bug, and prey on larger insects such as grasshoppers, beetles, and moths. Wheel bugs kill their victims within 30 seconds.

🐜 Using its needle-like beak, a wheel bug stabs its prey with poison, which dissolves their insides. Then it sucks up their body fluids through its straw-like mouthparts.

🐜 The beady, round eyes of the wheel bug are useful for spotting prey. Its long front legs seize and hold its victims tightly.

The female wheel bug lays 40 to 200 tiny eggs, which hatch into red and black nymphs, or young. The nymphs do not have wings or a wheel-like crest.

Wheel bugs produce chirping sounds by rubbing the tip of their beak against ridges under the front of their body. This may help them to communicate with other wheel bugs.

The wheel bug gives off a strong scent if it is disturbed. If predators smell it, they usually keep away.

Fact file

Lives: North and Central America

Habitat: Meadows and woodlands

Length: 1–1½ in/25–36 mm (adult); less than ¼ in/3 mm (nymph)

Lifecycle: 8 months

Diet: Insects

Rusty-patched bumblebee

Bombus affinis

- Rusty-patched bumblebees live together in colonies of up to a thousand bees, in underground nests.

- The workers and male bumblebees have a rusty-red patch of hair in the middle of their abdomen.

- The queen bee is leader of the colony, which also contains lots of female workers and some male bees.

- Only the queen bee lays eggs. After the eggs hatch, the baby bees take five weeks to develop into adults. Some will be new queens.

- In autumn, most of the colony dies. Only the new queens survive by sleeping underground. In spring, they lay eggs to start new colonies.

- Rusty-patched bumblebees have short tongues. They make holes in the sides of long-tubed flowers to reach the sweet nectar inside.

- In cold weather, rusty-patched bumblebees shiver to warm up their flight muscles so that they can fly.

- Disease, pesticides, habitat loss, and climate change all threaten the rusty-patched bumblebee. Conservationists and farmers are working hard to save the species.

Fact file

Lives: Eastern North America

Habitat: Grasslands, open woods, marshes, sand dunes, farmland, parks, and gardens

Length: ¼–½ in/10–16 mm (worker); ¾–1 in/20–22 mm (queen)

Lifecycle: 3 to 5 months

Diet: Flower pollen and nectar

Seven-spot ladybird

Coccinella septempunctata

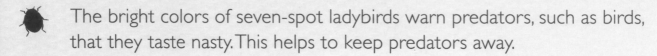 The bright colors of seven-spot ladybirds warn predators, such as birds, that they taste nasty. This helps to keep predators away.

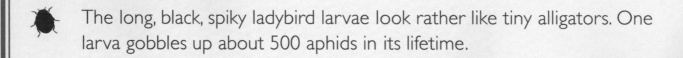 The seven-spot ladybird uses two pincers near its mouth to bite into a tasty meal of aphids, or greenfly, which are its favorite food. One ladybird can eat up to 50 aphids in a day, and more than 5,000 aphids in a lifetime.

The long, black, spiky ladybird larvae look rather like tiny alligators. One larva gobbles up about 500 aphids in its lifetime.

Fact file

Lives: Europe, Middle East, Asia, Africa, North America

Habitat: Grassland, woodland, gardens, parks, farmland

Length: About ¼ in/6–8 mm (adult); ½ in/12 mm (larva)

Lifecycle: 1 to 2 years

Diet: Aphids, scale insects, other soft-bodied insects

The ladybird keeps its fragile wings folded away under its red wing cases. It lifts the wing cases up and out of the way when it is flying.

If a ladybird is threatened, it squirts a horrible, smelly yellow liquid from its leg joints. Another of its tricks is to keep still and pretend to be dead. Predators ignore a "dead" ladybird because they prefer to eat living prey.

Over the winter, ladybirds gather together and go into a deep sleep called hibernation. They hibernate in hollow trees, under rocks, in piles of leaves, or in houses, attics, or sheds.

Devil's flower mantis

Idolomantis diabolica

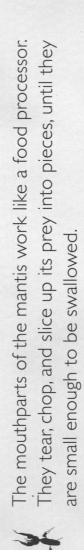

- This mantis is a master of disguise. It looks like a devil's flower orchid. It sits very still on the orchid, waiting for insects to visit the flower. Then it grabs them with its spiny front legs.

- The mouthparts of the mantis work like a food processor. They tear, chop, and slice up its prey into pieces, until they are small enough to be swallowed.

- At birth, a baby devil's flower mantis is black and shiny. Predators mistake it for an ant and avoid it, because real ants have a painful sting.

- Young devil's flower mantises are called nymphs. It is hard for predators to spot them because they look like dead brown leaves.

- Devil's flower mantis nymphs shed their skins seven or eight times as they grow bigger.

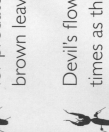

When it is threatened, the mantis raises its body and its front legs, and sways back and forth. This shows off its bright colors and makes it look bigger and more scary.

Adult males have huge, feathery antennae, or feelers. They use their antennae to pick up the scent of females that are ready to mate.

Fact file

Lives: East Africa

Habitat: Tropical grassland

Length: 4–5 in/10–13 cm

Lifecycle: 1 to 1¼ years

Diet: Flies, moths, butterflies, beetles, bees

Soil Termite

Macrotermes gilvus

- Soil termites build sturdy nest mounds of soil and chewed wood, glued together with saliva and droppings. The mounds can be 6½ feet (2 meters) high, which is the same height as a very tall person.

- Up to 60,000 termites may live in a single large nest mound.

- Soldier termites defend the nest. Workers look after the nest and young, as well as collecting and growing food. The queen termite lays eggs.

- Termites have a soft outer covering that dries up easily. This is why they live in dark, warm, damp nests, and are active at night when the air is moist. At night, they are safer from predators, too.

- Inside the termite nest, the pale-colored workers grow mushrooms in a "fungus garden," made up of chewed-up plants and droppings. The garden has a honeycomb shape, and can be as big as a football.

- Soldier and worker termites have weak eyesight and use their senses of touch and smell to check out their surroundings.

Fact file

Lives: Southeast Asia

Habitat: Forests and grasslands

Length: ¼ in/6 mm– ½ in/10 mm (soldier); ¼ in/5 mm (worker); 2½ in/60 mm (queen)

Lifecycle: 1 to 2 years (workers, soldiers); 10 to 25 years (queen)

Diet: Wood, leaves, mushrooms

Puss moth caterpillar

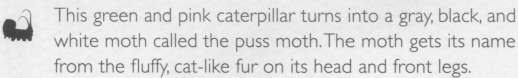

Cerura vinula

- This green and pink caterpillar turns into a gray, black, and white moth called the puss moth. The moth gets its name from the fluffy, cat-like fur on its head and front legs.

- The puss moth caterpillar has a patch of dark color on its back. This helps to break up the caterpillar's shape, making it hard to see as it feeds on green leaves.

- If it is alarmed, the caterpillar tries to look scary. It shows off the two fake "eyes" on its pink "face" and waves the two long, whip-like threads on its tail.

Fact file

Lives: Europe, Asia, northern Africa

Habitat: Woodland, parks, gardens

Length: 2¼–3 in/6–8 cm

Lifecycle: 30 to 35 weeks; 1 to 2 months (caterpillar only)

Diet: Willow and poplar leaves

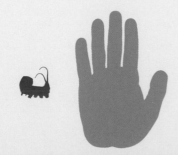

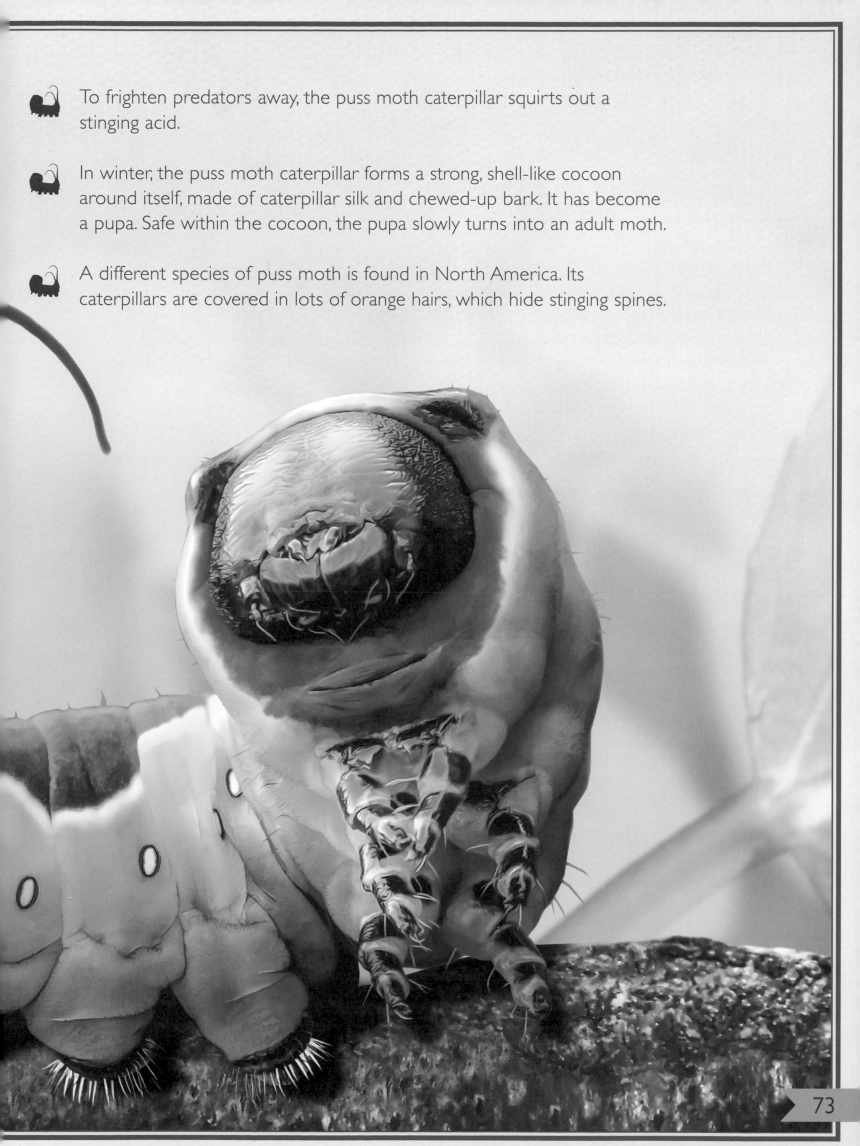

To frighten predators away, the puss moth caterpillar squirts out a stinging acid.

In winter, the puss moth caterpillar forms a strong, shell-like cocoon around itself, made of caterpillar silk and chewed-up bark. It has become a pupa. Safe within the cocoon, the pupa slowly turns into an adult moth.

A different species of puss moth is found in North America. Its caterpillars are covered in lots of orange hairs, which hide stinging spines.

Eastern dobsonfly

Corydalus cornutus

 Adult eastern dobsonflies are mainly active at night. They live for only a few days because all they need to do is mate and lay their eggs.

 The males use their horn-like mouthparts in jousting fights with rival males. They also use their "horns" when they want to impress females.

 Female eastern dobsonflies lay clusters of up to one thousand eggs on tree branches and rocks near fast-flowing water.

 The dobsonfly's eggs are covered in a white material. This makes them look like bird droppings, so predators leave them alone. The white coating also reflects heat and keeps the eggs cool.

Fact file

Lives: Eastern North America

Habitat: Rocky streams and rivers

Length: 3–5 in/75–140 mm (adult); 2¾–3½ in/70–90 mm (larva)

Lifespan: 1 year 5 weeks to 3 years 7 weeks

Diet: Insects, worms, shellfish (larva); flower nectar (adult female)

Eastern dobsonfly grubs, or larvae, can breathe both in and out of the water. They take in oxygen from water through feathery gills on their sides. On land, they breathe in air through holes called spiracles.

Great raft spider

Dolomedes plantarius

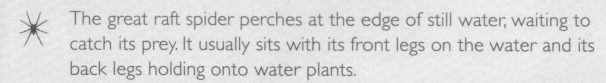

* The great raft spider perches at the edge of still water, waiting to catch its prey. It usually sits with its front legs on the water and its back legs holding onto water plants.

* Sensitive hairs on this spider's legs detect the vibrations made by its prey. It runs over the surface, or dives underwater to catch its victim.

* The great raft spider's long legs help to spread its weight on the water's surface and stop it sinking. Its feet make little hollows in the water, but the surface does not give way.

* To avoid predators, the spider can hide underwater for up to an hour. It breathes from air bubbles trapped in its body hairs.

* As part of his courtship display, the male great raft spider taps on the water's surface with his legs. When he gets close to a female, they both bob up and down in a courtship dance.

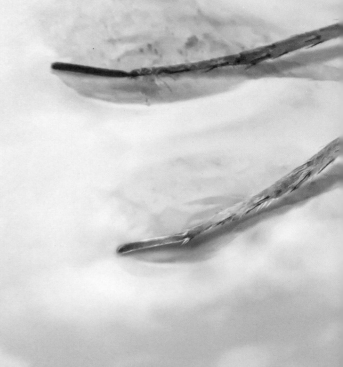

Fact file

Lives: Europe

Habitat: Wetlands

Legspan: up to 2¾ in/70 mm (female); up to 1¾ in/45 mm (male)

Lifespan: 2½ years

Diet: Insects, small fish, tadpoles

The egg sac of the female spider contains several hundred eggs. She carries the sac around for about three weeks. She dips it in the water to keep her eggs cool and stop them from drying out.

 The female great raft spider builds a silk tent called a nursery web for the baby spiders to live in. She guards the nursery web for about a week until the baby spiders, called spiderlings, are ready to live on their own.

Luna moth

Actias luna

- This giant moth will only just fit on your hand! Its wings measure up to 4 in (10 cm) from one wingtip to the other.

- "Luna" is another word for "moon," which is how this moth gets its name. The moon-like eyespots on its wings startle predators and draw their attention away from the moth's juicy body.

- These moths are also known as American moon moths. They fly at night and are most active when the moon is high in the sky.

- The luna moth is well camouflaged. Its green wings blend in with leafy backgrounds, and the red-brown edges of its front wings look like twigs with tiny buds growing from them.

- To find moths in the dark, bats send out sounds that echo back off the moths' bodies. The long tails of luna moths scatter these sounds in all directions, making it harder for bats to find and eat them.

- Luna moth caterpillars are eating machines. They increase their weight more than 4,000 times during their short lives of just three to six weeks.

- Adult luna moths do not eat anything. They survive by using the energy from fat stores built up when they were caterpillars.

- If the luna moth caterpillars are threatened by a bird or other predator, they make a clicking sound with their mouthparts. They also spit out a liquid with a horrible taste.

Fact file

Lives: North America, Mexico

Habitat: Deciduous forests

Length: 3 in/76 mm (adult);
2¾–3½ in/70–90 mm (caterpillar)

Lifecycle: 3 to 11½ months

Diet: Tree leaves (caterpillar)

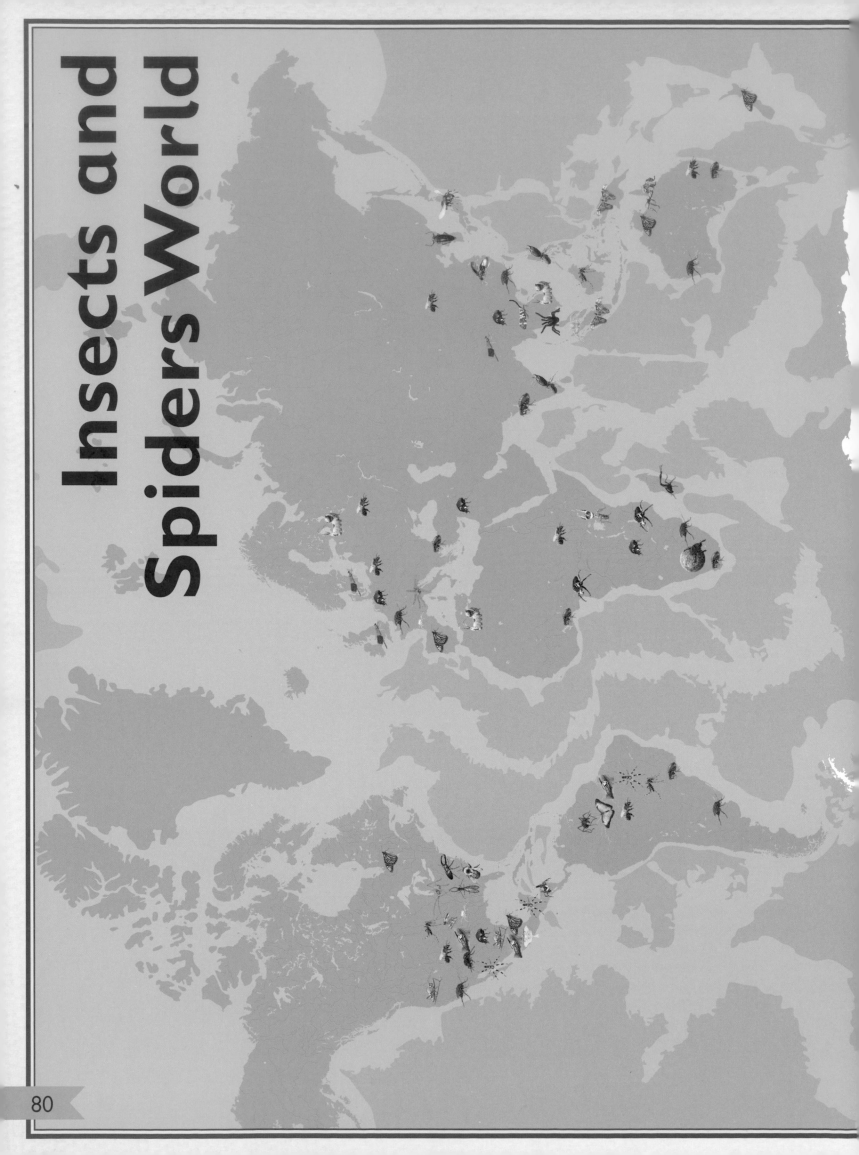

Insects and Spiders World